FLYING LOW
WITH

BROOM-HILDA #4

by Russell Myers

tempo
books

GROSSET & DUNLAP
A FILMWAYS COMPANY
Publishers • New York

LOOK OUT!

Broom-Hilda is on the loose and heading your way. You know what that means: side-splitting laughter that will wash away your blues. In addition to Irwin the troll, Gaylord the intellectual buzzard, and Grelber the master of insult, you'll meet some more of Broom-Hilda's coven in this volume of irresistible cartoons. Look for Marshall the vampire, who's searching for someone with ghoul-aid in the veins, and the cultured barbarians who, unlike Broom-Hilda, wouldn't lower themselves to watch the TV soaps.

RUSSELL
MYERS

11/4

11/5